teach me about

The Doctor

Copyright © Joy Berry, 2022
Originally Published, 1986

All rights are reserved.

No part of this book can be duplicated or used without the prior written permission of the copyright owner, except for the use of brief quotations from the book.

For inquiries or permission requests contact the publisher.

Published by Joy Berry Enterprises
www.joyberryenterprises.com

teach me about

The Doctor

By JOY BERRY

Illustrated by Bartholomew

My doctor is a woman.

I am going to visit my doctor

to find out whether or not

I am healthy and growing.

I go to the doctor's office to

see my doctor.

I have to wait in the waiting room until it is my turn to see the doctor.

The nurse is a person who helps the doctor.

The nurse measures me to see how tall I am.

She weighs me to see how heavy I am.

The nurse takes me to a smaller room.

There are many things in this room.

I take off my clothes so the doctor can see all of me.

Soon the doctor comes into the room to see me. She shines a little light into my eyes, ears, nose, and mouth. She presses my tongue down with a flat stick and asks me to say, "Ahhhh."

The doctor uses a special tool to listen to my heart and lungs. She asks me to take some deep breaths while she is listening.

The doctor tickles the bottom of my feet.

She taps my knee with a small rubber hammer.

She taps my elbow and other places, too.

The doctor gently feels my neck, arms, and tummy.

She gently thumps my chest.

The doctor also looks at other parts of my body.

The doctor puts a thin glass stick under my tongue.
She asks me to keep it there for a little while.

The doctor puts her fingertips on my wrist.

She looks at her watch while she is touching my wrist.

The doctor wraps a cloth around my arm and puffs it up with air.

Then she lets the air out of the cloth.

The doctor moves her finger. She asks me to watch her finger without moving my head. Then she asks me to look at a picture with letters or numbers on it and tell her what I see.

The doctor asks me to

- stretch,
- bend,
- stand up straight,
- walk, and
- sit.

She watches me while I do these things.

Sometimes the doctor asks me to go pee pee into a cup. Sometimes she takes a drop of blood out of my finger.

Sometimes the doctor gives me medicine to eat.

Other times the doctor puts the medicine into my arm or bottom with a needle.

The doctor is finished seeing me.

I get dressed.

I will not see her again for a long time unless I get sick or hurt.

If I get sick or hurt, I will go see my doctor.

She will help me get well.

helpful hints for parents about
The Doctor

Dear Parents:

The purpose of this book is
- to give children the information they need about the doctor in order to dispel the fears that are created by "not knowing," and
- to give children control by encouraging and showing them how to become active participants in their visits to the doctor.

You can best implement the purpose of this book by
- reading it to your child, and
- reading the following *Helpful Hints* and using them whenever applicable.

MEDICAL CARE

Regular medical care for your baby begins with prenatal care and should be continued throughout infancy and childhood.

Choosing a health practitioner

Before your baby's delivery, choose the type of regular medical care that's right for you. Your choices for infant/child medical care include, but are not limited to, the following:

- **Visiting or public health nurse.** These highly trained medical professionals will visit the mother and newborn several times in the weeks following delivery. Besides monitoring the health and well-being of both mother and baby, the visiting nurse can answer questions and give instructions in infant care.
- **Family or general practice physician.** These doctors specialize in the practice of general medicine for all members of the family. Some parents may prefer the advantage of seeing one doctor for both parents' and children's health needs.
- **Pediatrician.** These doctors specialize in the practice of pediatric medicine for infants, children, and adolescents. Some parents may prefer a doctor who specializes in children's health.
- **Well-baby clinic.** These health facilities are generally available through city or county health departments. Your state's department of health can provide a local referral. Regular examinations and immunizations are provided by qualified medical personnel at reduced cost or free for infants and children. The well-baby clinic provides health maintenance but does not provide diagnosis or treatment of illness or injury.

Choosing a medical doctor

To choose a doctor (pediatrician or family practitioner) for your child, ask for a referral from one or more of the following:

- your obstetrician or the doctor or midwife who delivered your baby:
- your local (city, county) medical society:
- a friend or relative who has a firsthand recommendation:
- the chief of staff of your local hospital.

To make your selection of a doctor, do the following:
- Decide on several criteria that you will require in your child's doctor.
- Make a check list of your criteria. These may include the following:
  1. doctor's experience
  2. length of practice
  3. availability in emergencies
  4. convenience of office location
  5. child-rearing philosophy
  6. rapport with your child
  7. rapport with parents
- Arrange an interview visit with the prospective doctor. Be sure to specify that you wish an interview, not a standard office visit.
- Take your child along for the interview if you think you can manage or if a co-parent can accompany you. This meeting provides an opportunity for your child to interact with the doctor in a nonthreatening situation. During the interview, do the following:
  1. Ask both specific questions and open-ended questions which will provide the information necessary to make your choice.
  2. Ask permission to take notes on the doctor's responses to your questions.
  3. Try to be brief and to the point.
  4. Observe your child's response to the doctor and vice versa.
- Evaluate the doctor on the basis of both your criteria *and* your intuition.

CONSULTING YOUR DOCTOR

Request an appointment with your doctor for your child's health examinations, illness, or injury.

Health examinations

Your child should have regular health examinations from birth through adolescence. These examinations generally include:
- height and weight measurements;
- physical examination, including eyes, ears, nose throat, heart, lungs, abdomen, back, and limb function, and skin and hair condition;

- growth and developmental evaluation;
- immunizations;
- health maintenance, such as medication, vitamin supplements, and nutritional recommendations.

Your doctor or health professional will provide a schedule for recommended visits and inoculations for the first six years. Generally, a recommended health examination schedule is as follows:

- two examinations in the first to the sixth week;
- every two months for the first six months;
- every three months from six months to two years;
- annually from age two to six years;
- annually or every two years (according to physician's preference) from six years through adolescence.

Helpful hints for health examination visits:

- Plan the appointment to fit into your child's routine of eating, napping, and bathing. A tired or hungry baby will not feel cooperative during the examination.
- Dress your child as simply and as lightly as the weather permits. Clothes that are easily removed should be chosen over baby's "best" outfit.
- Prepare a bag of items to carry into the examination visit for the baby or young child, such as:
  1. a change of clothes
  2. two fresh diapers
  3. light blanket for covering your undressed baby
  4. a doll or stuffed animal
  5. amusements for waiting
- Compile a list of questions, concerns, problems, and requests.
- Include a note pad to jot down your doctor's responses. Be sure to ask for more explanation if you don't understand the doctor's recommendations. Don't leave the office with unanswered questions.

Illness or injury

Ask about your doctor's policies regarding illness and injury emergencies. If your child becomes ill or is injured, telephone your doctor for instructions or an appointment. If the symptoms or the injury are serious, take your child directly to the nearest hospital emergency room.

If your child becomes ill, call your doctor for an appointment or advice.

Be prepared to give the following information to the doctor when you call. Tell the doctor your
- name,
- child's name,
- child's age,
- child's present temperature,
- child's present symptoms (include physical appearance, mood, sleep pattern, and eating pattern),
- pharmacist's name and telephone number, and
- child's allergies to any medication.

Your child's comfort and treatment and the alleviation of parental anxiety are the most important considerations during a visit to the doctor with a sick or injured child.

Consider the following:
- Try to have another adult transport and accompany you to the doctor so that you can give your full attention to your child.
- Avoid the waiting room by phoning ahead to determine the waiting time, and request to use an emergency entrance.
- Don't be alarmed if some of your child's symptoms disappear in the presence of the doctor. Your doctor should address the symptoms which you have observed and listed, answer your questions, and calm your fears.

Consult a second professional opinion if you are not satisfied with your doctor's diagnosis or treatment of your child or if the recommendation for treatment is serious, such as surgery or hospitalization.

PREPARE YOUR CHILD

Before the examination

Prepare your child for routine medical examinations by doing the following:
- Inform your child well in advance of the visit to the doctor.

- Answer your child's questions simply and honestly, alleviating fear by providing information.
- Play doctor to familiarize your child with the examination and what to expect from the doctor. Use a doll or stuffed animal as the "patient."
- Encourage your child to ask the doctor questions. Express any concerns on your child's behalf if your child has shared with you but won't share with the doctor. "Represent" your child to the doctor.

In the waiting room

To keep your child occupied and minimize fear, provide entertainment. Pack small items for amusement in a tote bag, a three-pound coffee can with a plastic lid, or a large purse with many compartments. Avoid toys that could be noisy, messy, or intrusive to others.

The examination

Involve your child as much as possible in the doctor's examination.
- Have the doctor talk *to* the child as well as the parent. The dialogue should be child centered.
- Ask the doctor to inform the child about what to expect and which instruments will be used.
- Use a doll or stuffed animal for demonstration purposes if necessary.
- Encourage your child to ask questions.
- Never leave your child alone with the doctor.
- Hold your child on your lap during the examination if he or she is frightened.
- Cover your undressed child with a blanket or robe if the examining room is cool.
- Be sure the doctor answers all of your child's questions honestly, accurately, and with sensitivity.

AFTER THE DOCTOR'S VISIT

Follow-up treatment

Involve your child in the treatment or the doctor's recommendations. If medicine or supplements are prescribed, use a colorful sticker chart to track and reward progress.

Reward
Make the visit to the doctor a positive experience by combining it with a happy activity afterward. Let the child know that there will be a reward *before* the visit so he or she can look forward to it. A stop at a playground on the way home creates a positive association.

ADDITIONAL INFORMATION

Locating a doctor away from home
If you need a doctor for your child while traveling or visiting out of town, it is most likely because of a medical emergency. Telephone the best hospital in the area, and ask for a recommendation from the staff pediatrician or family practice specialist. If the condition does not require emergency attention, avoid using the emergency room of an unfamiliar hospital. Be sure to carry your health insurance card when you travel.

Hospitals
- Arrange a field trip with your child to the hospital. Visit the emergency room, have lunch in the cafeteria, and tour the hospital gift shop. Hopefully, this pleasant experience will give your child a positive attitude toward hospitals, diffuse anxiety, and make him or her more receptive and cooperative during hospitalization or emergency treatment.
- Remember that parents have a legal right to stay nights as well as days with their hospitalized children. If you choose to do this, you may want to share the responsibility with a co-parent.
- Help your hospitalized child feel comfortable and secure by allowing him or her to bring favorite things from home (for example, a toy, a doll, a blanket, a pillow).
- Stack wrapped surprises on your child's bedside table. Let your child open one package on each day of his or her hospital stay. Try to include items and activities that are suitable to use in the hospital.
- Let friends and relatives know exactly when and where your child is in the hospital. Encourage them to write or visit your child.